My First Adventures/Mis primeras aventuras

MY FIRST TRIP TO THE DENTIST/ MI PRIMERA VISITA AL DENTISTA

By Katie Kawa / Traducción al español: Eduardo Alamán

Gareth Stevens
Publishing

Please visit our website, www.garethstevens.com. For a free color catalog of all our high-quality books, call toll free 1-800-542-2595 or fax 1-877-542-2596.

Library of Congress Cataloging-in-Publication Data

Kawa, Katie.
My first trip to the dentist = Mi primera visita al dentista / Katie Kawa.
    p. cm. — (My first adventures = Mis primeras aventuras)
Includes index.
ISBN 978-1-4339-6627-9 (library binding)
1. Dentistry—Juvenile literature. 2. Children—Preparation for dental care—Juvenile literature. I. Title.
RK63.K393 2012
617.0083—dc23
                                        2011031665

First Edition

Published in 2012 by
Gareth Stevens Publishing
111 East 14th Street, Suite 349
New York, NY 10003

Copyright © 2012 Gareth Stevens Publishing

Editor: Katie Kawa
Designer: Haley W. Harasymiw
Spanish Translation: Eduardo Alamán

All Illustrations by Planman Technologies

Printed in the United States of America

CPSIA compliance information: Batch #CW12GS: For further information contact Gareth Stevens, New York, New York at 1-800-542-2595.

Contents

Contenido

Today I am going
to the dentist.

Hoy, voy a ir al dentista.

5

The dentist keeps
my teeth healthy.

El dentista mantiene mis
dientes sanos.

7

A man helps my dentist.
He cleans my teeth.

El dentista tiene un
ayudante. El ayudante
me limpia los dientes.

He brushes them.

El ayudante me cepilla
los dientes.

He takes a picture
of my teeth.
This is called an X-ray.

Toma una foto de mis
dientes. A esto se le
llama radiografía.

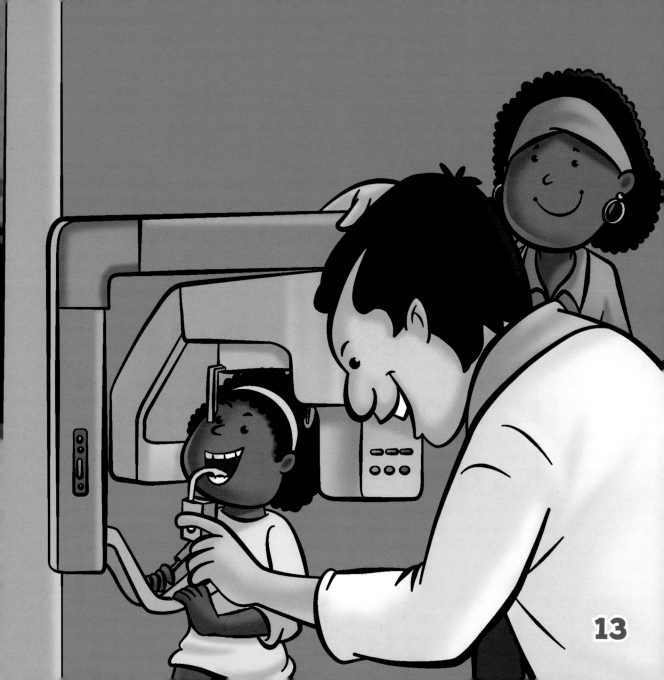

13

Then I see the dentist.
She looks at my teeth.

Luego veo a la dentista.
La dentista me revisa
los dientes.

15

She counts them too.

También cuenta
mis dientes.

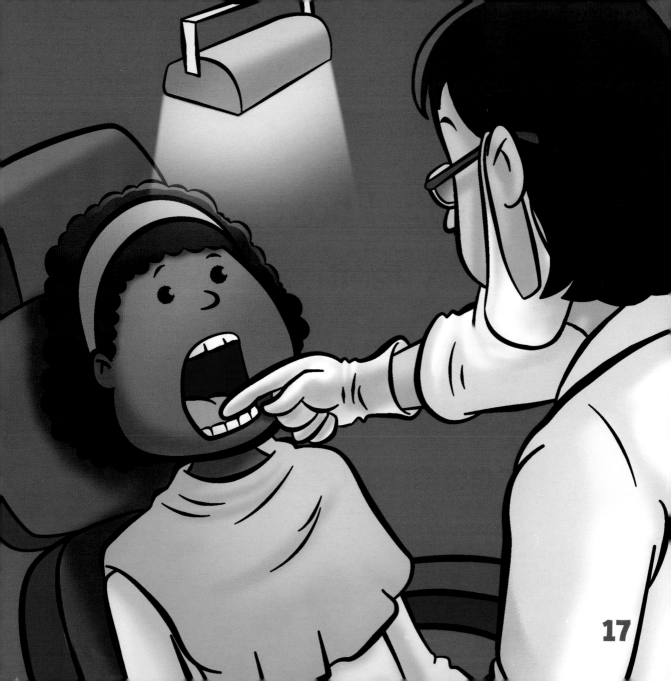

She says I have
healthy teeth.

La dentista dice que
tengo una boca sana.

19

She gives me a sticker!

¡Y me da una pegatina!

I love my clean teeth!

¡Me encanta tener los dientes limpios!

23

Words to Know/
Palabras que debes saber

sticker/
(la) pegatina

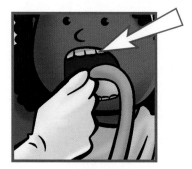

teeth/
(los) dientes

Index / Índice